Grades 6 up

PRIMARY SOURCES OF POLITICAL SYSTEMS™

DICTATORSHIP
A PRIMARY SOURCE ANALYSIS

ROSE McCARTHY

rosen central
Primary Source

The Rosen Publishing Group, Inc., New York

Published in 2005 by The Rosen Publishing Group, Inc.
29 East 21st Street, New York, NY 10010

Copyright © 2005 by The Rosen Publishing Group, Inc.

First Edition

Library of Congress Cataloging-in-Publication Data

McCarthy, Rose.
Dictatorship : a primary source analysis / Rose McCarthy.— 1st ed.
    p. cm.— (Primary sources of political systems)
Includes bibliographical references and index.
Contents: Caesar and the Roman dictatorship—The French Revolution and Napoleon's reign—Adolf Hitler: The Führer of Nazi Germany—The Communist dictatorships—Franco and Fascism in Spain—Three dictators of the Americas.
ISBN 0-8239-4519-7
1. Dictators—Europe—Biography. 2. Dictators—Caribbean Area—Biography.
3. Dictators—South America—Biography. 4. Despotism. [1. Dictators. 2. Despotism.
3. World politics.]
I. Title. II. Series.
D107.B74 2004
321.9'092'2—dc22
                                                                            2003015247

Manufactured in the United States of America

On the cover: Francisco Franco delivering an address in Madrid, Spain, in 1839.

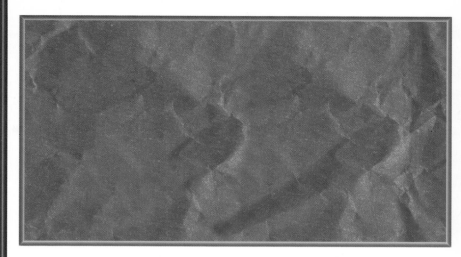

CONTENTS

INTRODUCTION

A dictator is a ruthless leader who holds complete control over the government of his country. A dictator may seize power or he may inherit it. Sometimes, he is elected by the people. A dictator often rules even when the people would prefer a different leader or form of government.

Sometimes, a dictator rises to power in a time of crisis. The people rally behind him, hoping that he will bring stability back to their lives. They expect that he will return fair and just rule to the land. But a dictator holds on to control after the crisis is past. Napoléon Bonaparte pulled France from the chaos of the French Revolution in 1804. Augusto Pinochet staged a military coup in Chile in 1973 after his predecessor's policies brought on an economic crisis and a near state of revolt among Chileans. Both became dictators rather than return the government to the people.

Sometimes, a charismatic dictator wins the devotion of the people. He can persuade the people that he has their best interests at heart. Dictators usually repress opposition using a combination of charisma, intimidation, and force. Adolf Hitler rose to power by

This undated photograph shows Chilean dictator Augusto Pinochet reviewing troops inside the presidential palace in Santiago, Chile. Pinochet ruled as president and commander of the armed forces between 1973 and 1990.

persuading many Germans to believe his point of view but held on to power by terrorizing people who challenged him.

A dictator usually controls a country's army, police, government branches, and justice system. In the twentieth century, many dictators put totalitarian systems into place. In totalitarian governments, dictators aim to control every aspect of people's lives. Changing the laws of the country, they create police states. Dictators often use secret police to terrorize the population. By doing so, they create such a climate of fear that they stifle dissent and discourage revolt.

The dictator abolishes other branches of government and bans all political parties except his own. He crushes those who oppose him. The dictator might impose curfews and censorship, and he might dictate the subject matter taught in schools.

Dictatorships have existed since ancient times. Many countries have succeeded in getting rid of their dictators and adopting democratic systems. But as long as injustice, instability, and corruption exist within governments, particularly in poor countries, there is a risk of crises developing into opportunities for a dictator to seize power.

CHAPTER ONE

CAESAR AND THE ROMAN DICTATORSHIP

This is a bronze sesterce, a roman coin. A likeness of Caesar is on one side of the coin. The other side bears one of his most well-known statements: "Veni, vidi, vici," which means "I came, I saw, I conquered."

Gaius Julius Caesar (100–44 BC) was born during a turbulent time in Roman history. Four hundred years earlier, in 510 BC, the citizens of the Italian city of Rome created a system of government called a republic, which enabled Roman citizens to vote for their leaders.

Throughout the centuries, the Romans conquered their neighbors until they ruled a sprawling empire. Rome came to dominate the lands surrounding the Mediterranean Sea. As it expanded, the Roman Republic descended into a state of turmoil. The system of government had been intended to govern a city, not a vast empire.

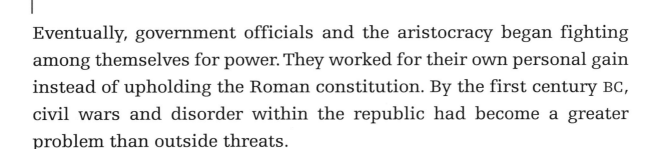

Eventually, government officials and the aristocracy began fighting among themselves for power. They worked for their own personal gain instead of upholding the Roman constitution. By the first century BC, civil wars and disorder within the republic had become a greater problem than outside threats.

Rome's Constitutional Dictatorship

According to the Roman constitution, the Senate and three people's assemblies governed the republic. Other elected officials, such as consuls, tribunes, quaestors, and censors, saw to the administration of the country. Although the constitution aimed to prevent any single person from gaining control of the republic, it created the office of dictator.

One of Rome's two consuls could appoint a dictator during a time of emergency, such as war or internal struggles. It would have been difficult for the Senate and other oversized governmental bodies to govern during a crisis that required quick decisions and quick actions. The dictator served, with some limits, as supreme ruler during such times. He was exempt from some Roman laws, and most of his orders could not be challenged. The dictator could not, however, change the constitution, declare war, or control the treasury. Rome's dictators would serve for six months. Between 501 BC and 44 BC, when the office was abolished, there were eighty-eight dictators in Rome.

In his massive *History of Rome*, the great historian Livy (64 or 59 BC–17 AD) wrote about the rise of the legendary dictator Lucius Quinctius Cincinnatus. Cincinnatus became dictator in 458 and 439 BC to battle Rome's enemies. On both occasions, Cincinnatus resigned his dictatorship and went home to his farm after he returned from battle.

The balance of power among Rome's governing bodies had shifted by the time Caesar was born. The Senate gained control over the assemblies, consuls, tribunes, and other official groups. All senators were wealthy landowners, and many belonged to aristocratic families that had held senatorial seats for centuries. They violently put down anyone who challenged their authority. At the same time, wars had hurt the economy and taken away the livelihoods and homes of many peasants. Many Romans were unhappy with the Senate's corrupt rule.

This reproduction of a painting by S. J. Ferris depicts Julius Caesar standing on the bow of a ship with a knife in each hand during his invasion of England in 55 BC.

In 83 BC, a general named Lucius Cornelius Sulla (138–78 BC) changed Roman politics forever by raising his own army and leading it into Rome to rid the Senate of his political enemies. Ruthlessly revising the constitution, he led a reign of terror against all opposition. He took absolute control of Rome in 82 BC and ruled until 80 BC. His reforms did not last, but he set an example by raising an army and establishing a dictatorship. Young Julius Caesar would learn from his example. Caesar, however, would combine political savvy and charisma with brute force to become a formidable statesman as well as a supreme ruler.

The Dictatorship of Julius Caesar

Caesar came from a well-to-do but not wealthy family. He joined the army at age eighteen and involved himself in politics upon arriving home. At age thirty, he became a magistrate and thus a member of the Senate and continued to rise in power and office. Through political maneuvering, he formed a triumvirate, a group of three rulers, with the great general Pompey and the wealthy Crassus. The three came to dominate the Roman government.

In 58 BC, Caesar left Rome to begin a military campaign against the Gallic tribes outside the Roman Empire in the area we know today as France. He led the military to triumph in 52 BC. By then, Crassus had died and Pompey had turned against Caesar. The Senate wanted Caesar put on trial for abuses of power. Caesar's army invaded Rome, sparking a civil war.

Pompey led the forces against Caesar. Caesar's men won a decisive victory, and Pompey fled to Egypt. Caesar followed. Upon arrival, he found that King Ptolemy XIII had already killed Pompey. When Caesar returned to Rome in 47 BC, he arranged triumphant celebrations and eventually coerced the Senate into making him dictator for an unprecedented ten-year term.

Caesar faced a daunting task. The civil war had left the Roman government in shambles. Caesar planned ambitious building projects to give work to the poor and to improve the city. A number of reforms helped veterans and poor Romans. He enacted a new calendar, the Julian calendar, which we still use today.

Caesar was an autocratic ruler who used his military command and his veto power as tribune to enforce his policies. He gave the appearance that he was working within the republic's political structure. In reality, he often just declared his decisions to the Senate and had them issued as senatorial decrees without a debate or vote. Intimidated, the Senate conferred numerous honors on him. Any senator who opposed these gestures risked removal from the Senate. Moreover, Caesar issued coins that bore his portrait and encouraged—sometimes demanded—rituals that resembled worship of the Roman gods or that treated him as if he were king. In 44 BC, Caesar forced the Senate to declare him dictator for life.

Caesar had brought peace to Rome, but he had not made peace with the Senate. A handful of senators plotted his death on March 15, 44 BC. March 15 was known as the Ides of March in the ancient Roman calendar. They struck as he presided over the Senate. According to the Roman historian Cassius Dio, "When the right moment came, one of them approached him, as if to express his thanks for some favour or other, and pulled his toga from his shoulder, thus giving the signal that had been agreed upon by the conspirators. Thereupon they attacked him from many sides at once and wounded him to death."

The senators failed to restore power to the Senate. The Roman Republic fell once again into war. Caesar's adopted son, Gaius

This undated engraving shows Vercingetorix, a Gallic tribal chief, surrendering to Julius Caesar in 52 BC. Vercingetorix's forces had mounted a valiant defense against Caesar's army.

Octavius Thurinus (63 BC–AD 14), eventually emerged as dictator. He proclaimed himself Caesar Augustus, emperor of Rome. From that time until its fall in 476 AD, Rome was ruled by dictators.

Documenting Caesar

We know about Julius Caesar's life and rule from a variety of sources. Caesar and his contemporaries left behind documents and records, many of which have survived to the present day. Greek and Roman historians wrote of Caesar's life and his role in changing the republic. Archaeologists have unearthed relics that give evidence about Caesar and the lives of typical Romans during his time.

Documents from the time describe Caesar's personality as well as the events of his life. The historians Suetonius (c. AD 69–c. 140) and Plutarch (c. AD 46–c. 120) both wrote biographies of Caesar. Cicero (106–43 BC), one of Rome's greatest lawyers and orators, depicted the politics and politicians of Rome in his essays and orations.

Caesar himself described his military campaigns. His *Conquest of Gaul* provides a detailed account of the battles against Rome's enemies. Some modern historians believe that Caesar's *The Civil Wars* exaggerates facts to impress the people and discredit his enemies.

All sources agree that Caesar was a brilliant military leader, a masterful politician, and a powerful orator. He had many powerful friends but also worked to make himself popular with the Roman people. Plutarch writes that the young Caesar "won a great and brilliant popularity by his eloquence as an advocate, and much good will from the common people for the friendliness of his manners in intercourse with them, since he was ingratiating beyond his years." Cassius Dio describes Caesar as a politician with a mild nature. However, he called for immediate punishment of his enemies.

CHAPTER TWO

THE FRENCH REVOLUTION AND NAPOLÉON'S REIGN

Many centuries after Caesar's rule, the world was to see another man rise through the ranks of politics and war to become a ruthless, history-making dictator. His name was Napoléon Bonaparte. He came to power in France during the chaotic aftermath of the French Revolution.

The French Revolution

On July 14, 1789, a mob stormed and took over the Bastille in Paris. An old fortress, the Bastille was a notorious prison where political prisoners were confined. To many of the French, it symbolized the injustice of King Louis XVI's

Napoléon on Horseback at the St. Bernard Pass, a painting by Jacques-Louis David in 1801, shows Napoléon in 1800 as he leads French forces against Austrian troops in Italy. It is one of the most famous depictions of the French dictator and emperor.

On July 14, 1789, the overburdened poor of Paris stormed the Bastille, an old fortress and prison. Determined to retrieve the gunpowder and weapons stored there, they met little resistance. Their success sparked many revolts throughout France and marked the beginning of the French Revolution.

government. As monarch, Louis XVI sat at the pinnacle of the French political structure. Below him, the society was divided into three estates, or classes. The First Estate was made up of the clergy. The Second Estate consisted of the nobility. The masses, 96 percent of the population, made up the Third Estate, which included merchants, farmers, and craftsmen, as well as peasants.

A number of factors contributed to the unrest that led to the French Revolution. The Third Estate was heavily taxed and had little political power. Even when members of the lower classes could barely support themselves, their taxes paid for the lavish lifestyles of the nobles and clergy. In addition, the monarchy had mismanaged the economy, creating a national debt. The king sought to impose new taxes, even on the first two estates.

Following the storming of the Bastille, representatives of the Third Estate created the National Assembly and invited members of the clergy and nobility to join. Winning the support of the popular mobs in Paris, the National Assembly was soon in a position to change the political structure of France. In the summer of 1789, the National Assembly passed the Declaration of the Rights of Man and of the Citizen. This document outlined the "inalienable rights" of citizens in a justly governed nation. The rights included liberty, the equality of all citizens in the eyes of the law, and freedom to communicate ideas and opinions, as well as the rights to own property and to resist oppression. The assembly based many of the points on the philosophy of the eighteenth century, especially the *Contrat Social* (Social Contract) by Jean-Jacques Rousseau (1712–1778). The assembly also drew on the American Declaration of Independence.

Robespierre and the Reign of Terror

It would be a long time before the French would enjoy these rights. In 1791, the National Assembly drew up a constitution that gave more power to the people but permitted a limited monarchy. Nonetheless, King Louis XVI felt threatened. He tried to flee the country, but he was

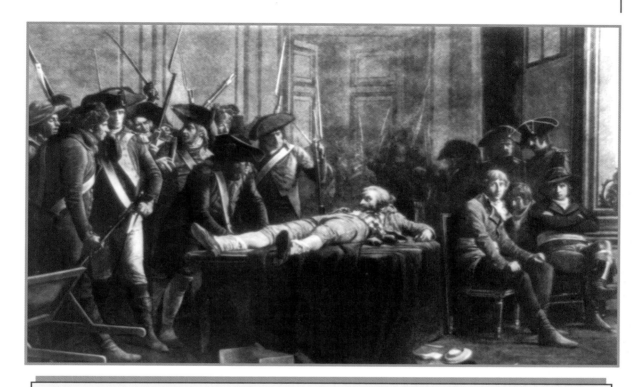

A leader in the French Revolution, Robespierre served briefly as France's temporary dictator, a notion inspired by the Romans. But Robespierre quickly lost favor. On July 27, 1794, Robespierre was arrested and interrogated, which this painting depicts. He and many of his supporters were executed by guillotine the next day.

caught and brought back as a prisoner. The constitution soon collapsed, and France declared war on Austria, which was trying to force the restoration of King Louis XVI to the throne. This was the first of a series of wars France fought against neighboring countries that were ruled by monarchs who feared the spread of Republican ideas.

The revolutionaries broke into rival factions. A group called the Girondins seized control of the French government in 1792 in an attempt to form a republic. They arrested many supporters of the king's. Mobs broke into the prison, killing 2,000 nobles and clergy. In January 1793, King Louis XVI was executed at the guillotine.

The Girondins were soon ousted, and a committee led by Maximilien Robespierre (1758–1794) formed a dictatorship. Robespierre's brief rule became known as the Reign of Terror. Ironically, before he took power, Robespierre fought against capital punishment. However, in a speech given in December 1793, he stated, "To good citizens revolutionary government owes the full protection of the state; to the enemies of the people it owes only death." He crushed all rebellions with military force and execution as he saw fit. Eighteen thousand people were executed at the guillotine, and more than 20,000 were killed by other means.

Joseph Fouché (1759–1820), who worked to topple Robespierre, describes him in his *Memoirs of Joseph Fouché, Duke of Otranto*, as "a man who combined cunning with pride, envy, hatred and vindictiveness; who had an unquenchable thirst for the blood of his colleagues and whose aptitude, bearing, cast of mind and obstinacy of character equipped him to rise to the most terrible occasions." Fouché and dissenters within the government turned against Robespierre. They arrested him and sent him to the guillotine on July 28, 1794.

The government was left in chaos. A constitution in 1795 established a five-member directory and a legislature. In 1797, the directors seized control of the government, relying on the military to uphold their corrupt and inept rule.

In 1799, Emmanuel-Joseph Sieyès (1748–1836), one of the early French revolutionaries, became a member of the directory. He wished desperately to restore some sort of order to the country. Napoléon Bonaparte (1769–1821) returned to France from a military campaign in October 1799 and was greeted as a hero. Sieyès approached Napoléon and enlisted his help in restoring a constitutional government.

Napoléon's Rise and Fall

Napoléon Bonaparte was born and raised in Corsica, an island acquired by France in 1768. He did not grow up with French traditions and history, and he did not learn the language until the age of nine. During the French Revolution, Napoléon held a more detached view of the leaders and events than did most Frenchmen.

In 1793, he joined the artillery and impressed his commanders. By 1794, he was a general. Shortly afterward, he was arrested for allegedly supporting Robespierre's faction. Although soon released, he lost his commission and slipped into poverty.

Military leaders remembered his ability, though, and soon gave him a position of high command. In 1895, he distinguished himself immediately by putting down a revolt in Paris. Boldly, he went on, invading Italy and then Egypt, becoming famous for his military brilliance.

Considered one of the world's great military leaders, Napoléon Bonaparte is a historical figure as well as a legend. His dramatic life has inspired writers, filmmakers, and playwrights. Their works, in turn, have contributed to the creation of the Napoleonic legend.

Napoléon agreed to aid Sieyès and a few other government officials in an attempt to overthrow the directory. He brought the backing of the army and successfully ousted the directory on November 9, 1799. Sieyès had drawn up a new constitution. Napoléon immediately changed it to concentrate power in his own hands.

From the beginning, Napoléon was an absolute ruler. At first, he established a three-member consulate, making himself first consul, which put him in control of all the power. In 1802, he became consul for life. Then in 1804, he crowned himself emperor.

Napoléon passed sweeping reforms that finally brought stability to France. He reorganized regional governments, set up a nationwide educational system, established the Bank of France, and created a new legal code. These reforms increased the power of the central government, thereby cementing Napoléon's command of public authority. His Napoleonic Code, addressing civil law, influenced law around the world. Through military force and treaties, he made peace with most of the nation's enemies.

Napoléon also established a vast police network that included a secret force and spies who monitored the activities of Napoléon's political enemies. Dissent was stifled, and the press was severely restricted. Influential people who criticized Napoléon's policies risked arrest, persecution, or exile.

However, Napoléon was a popular ruler. Although dictatorial, he preserved many of the progressive achievements of the French Revolution. These included abolishing special privileges for the aristocracy, granting civil equalities for religious minorities, and opening government positions to all people based on talent, rather than aristocratic birth. Moreover, he was widely revered by the French for being a brilliant military strategist.

While the French were generally satisfied with Napoléon's domestic policy, the rest of the world was troubled by his foreign policies. During his reign as emperor (1804–1814), Napoléon launched a number of wars that are today referred to as the Napoleonic Wars.

In 1805, the French military swept across Europe. Russia, Prussia, Poland, and Sweden fell to Napoléon's forces. France dominated most of Europe, with only Britain left unconquered. Each conquest made him more popular at home. Napoléon gave royal thrones and aristocratic holdings to his family members and favorite marshals. He also imposed onerous taxes on his conquests to finance more wars and his programs in France. Nevertheless, he introduced the positive reforms of the Napoleonic Code in the countries he conquered.

Within a few years, Napoléon's fortunes began to turn. After a disastrous invasion of Russia in 1812, his allies began to desert him. His enemies formed a coalition to oppose France and seized Paris in 1814. At the urging of the Senate, Napoléon abdicated the throne and went into exile on the island of Elba.

In 1815, he changed his mind and rallied the French behind him once again in a brief reign known as the Hundred Days. War broke out again, and Napoléon met his final downfall at the Battle of Waterloo. He died six years later in exile on the small island of St. Helena.

Many historians regard Napoléon as the first of the modern dictators. However, he did not systematically execute tens of thousands of his countrymen, like Robespierre before him or like many of the world's dictators after him. Nevertheless, he was responsible for the loss of an estimated 5 million lives during the Napoleonic Wars.

CHAPTER THREE

ADOLF HITLER: THE FÜHRER OF NAZI GERMANY

Adolf Hitler gives the stiff-armed Nazi salute at a Nazi Party congress in 1934. He rose from a poor peasant background to rule Germany and then to conquer most of Europe.

The political turmoil of the twentieth century produced its share of ruthless dictators. Among the most heinous and destructive was Germany's Adolf Hitler and his National Socialist German Workers Party, which was widely known as the Nazi Party.

Born in 1889, Hitler was a poor student and a failed artist. Having fought in World War I, he bitterly resented Germany's defeat. He declared that Germany would have won, had it not been "stabbed in the back" by German traitors. According to Hitler, cowards in the government, egged on by Jews and Communists, had surrendered, even though the army could have emerged victorious. He argued that these people needed to pay a price for the loss of German pride.

Many Germans, agreeing with his ideas, joined Hitler's Nazi Party, which was formed in 1920. In 1923, Hitler attempted a *putsch*, or an overthrow of the government, in a Munich beer hall. His plot failed, and he was arrested. Hitler wrote *Mein Kampf* while spending a term in prison for treason.

The Rise of Hitler and the Nazis

Mein Kampf presented a hodgepodge of Hitler's views and prejudices. While he did not put forth a clear ideology for his party, his rants against Jews appealed to many Germans who, like Hitler, were looking for a place to cast blame for their problems. *Mein Kampf* became the most important book in Hitler's Germany, which he termed the Third Reich, meaning that it was the third time in history that German states were united to form an empire. Released from prison in late 1924, Hitler immediately started rebuilding the Nazi Party.

The Nazis used propaganda to spread their ideas. Nazi propaganda relied on certain stereotypes. Slogans were repeated often to ensure that everyone grasped the ideas. Hitler presented only the information that was favorable to his side. Propaganda is designed to manipulate people's beliefs and emotions as well as sway their allegiance.

Support for the Nazis grew over the years. After a series of elections between 1930 and 1932, the Nazi Party held far more seats in the Reichstag, Germany's parliament, than any other political party. With such popular support, Hitler demanded to be appointed chancellor. He got his wish in January 1933, when German president Paul von Hindenburg appointed Hitler chancellor.

Within months, Hitler transformed Germany into a dictatorship. When a fire destroyed the Reichstag building a week before new elections were due, Hitler blamed the Communist Party. Concerned, President Hindenburg signed a decree authorizing the Nazis to suppress the political opposition. With this new authority, the Nazis arrested and intimidated members of the Communist and Social Democratic Parties. Hitler used his private army—called the storm troopers, or SA for short—to carry out the job.

In March 1933, Hitler convinced the parliament to pass the Enabling Act. This law placed all organizations under Nazi control. Immediately, the Nazis banned several parties and eventually, in July, declared Germany a one-party state. Hitler ordered that Communists, Socialists, and Jews be removed from their positions within the civil service and the court system. He reorganized local and state governments, giving key positions to Nazi activists and supporters. Hitler also replaced trade unions with Nazi organizations.

When President Hindenburg died in 1934, Hitler assumed his office, thereby combining the presidency and the chancellorship. In doing so, Hitler became both head of state and head of government, with, effectively, no check on his power. For the next eleven years, Hitler used terror and propaganda to maintain his control over Germany.

Hitler's Propaganda

The extensive information campaign that Hitler used to build the Nazi Party paled in comparison to the propaganda he would unleash as Germany's ruler. By nature, government propaganda tells people the perspective, sometimes including lies, of that government only. With the educational system, press, and cultural organizations firmly under their control, the Nazis infused their messages into virtually all areas of German life. In school, German children learned Nazi propaganda. At home or on the street, Germans of all ages were bombarded with Nazi messages on the radio or in posters.

The Nazis held fiery mass meetings to rally the people. Hitler and some of the other leaders were dynamic speakers. Hitler staged many elaborate events. The propagandist filmmaker Leni Riefenstahl used footage from a 1934 rally in Nuremberg, Germany, in which masses of uniformed men marched in support of Nazism, in her film *Triumph of the Will*. The rally was held only a few weeks after Hitler became führer, or leader, of Germany.

The Nazis were skilled at using propaganda to gain votes and support. This poster shows a man laying stones on a building as a Nazi flag flaps in the background. The poster promotes the purchase of German goods.

Hitler began his political career by rabble-rousing in beer halls for his fledgling political party. Hitler preached that the Germans hadn't lost World War I but had merely been removed from the international stage. This reasoning reignited dormant nationalism among the German people. In this photograph, Hitler addresses a huge Nazi rally in Dortmund, Germany, in 1933.

Hitler's Terror

Hitler ruthlessly persecuted his enemies and people he simply did not like or trust. No one was immune to his terror. To reduce the power of his own storm troopers, he murdered the group's leaders in 1933. He replaced it as his private army with the SS (Schutzstaffel, or Guard Detachment), under the leadership of Heinrich Himmler. Throughout his rule, the SS carried out many police arrests—first of Communists

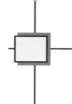

and Socialists, then later of Jews. Many Germans who opposed his policies left the country. However, most simply suppressed their opinions in public.

Hitler and the Jews

More than any other group, the Jewish people suffered under Hitler's rule. Along with the certainty of Aryan superiority he expressed in *Mein Kampf*, Hitler continually returned to his paranoid hatred of Jews. He told of his personal dislike of Jews from an early age. He outlined his belief that Jews conspired to control the press and world finances and that they contaminated the Aryan race. In his explanation of how Jews gradually gained power within societies, he described a backlash against Jews. This backlash would be a pale foreshadowing of Hitler's own treatment of the Jews.

The Nazis took actions against the Jews immediately upon gaining control of the government. In 1933, they created the first concentration camp in Dachau, where Jews and Hitler's political opponents were imprisoned, pressed into forced labor, and executed. At first, Nazis terrorized Jews and boycotted their businesses. Then the Nuremberg Laws of 1935 legally restricted Jews' rights. Jews could not be citizens of the Reich, and they could no longer vote or occupy public office. Jews could not marry non-Jewish Germans. Later, Jews were stripped of their livelihoods and forced from their homes. Many Jews fled Germany. Others could not believe the Nazis were such a threat that they should abandon their homeland. Many of those who stayed were eventually killed. The Nazis executed more than 6 million Jews in a systematic campaign of extermination, known as the Holocaust.

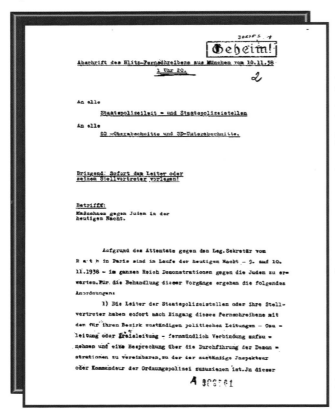

This November 10, 1938, telegram was written by Reinhard Heydrich, Nazi chief of the security police. It informed police departments throughout Germany to expect anti-Jewish demonstrations and instructed them to allow demonstrators to destroy Jewish homes and businesses. (Refer to page 55 for a partial transcription.)

German Expansion

Hitler was obsessed with Lebensraum, or "living space," for Germany. He stated in *Mein Kampf* that to continue to exist Germany needed to become an empire. Lebensraum meant acquiring colonies. Hitler's idea was to enlarge Germany by conquering its neighbors.

After Hitler came to power in 1933, he began to withdraw from international organizations and treaties. He built Germany's military into a massive force. In 1937, he annexed Austria, making it part of the German Reich. Two years later, he invaded and seized control of neighboring Czechoslovakia. European nations did not try to stop him, even though Great Britain and France had sworn to defend Czechoslovakia. Great Britain's prime minister, Neville Chamberlain, finally spoke out against Germany in a speech on March 16, 1939. He asked: "Is this the last attack upon a small State or is it to be followed by others? Is this, in effect, a step in the direction of an attempt to dominate the world by force?"

MUSSOLINI

Benito Mussolini became dictator of Italy in 1922. Mussolini suppressed opposition and outlawed trade unions and political parties, except his. He relied on propaganda emphasizing what was "good" for Italy to win public support. Mussolini allied Italy with Hitler during World War II. He lost power after he was captured during the war.

Chamberlain's question was soon answered. In August 1939, Hitler signed a nonaggression treaty with Joseph Stalin of the USSR (Union of Soviet Socialist Republics). Each country promised not to attack the other. Hitler had viewed the USSR as the only potential obstacle to his eastward expansion. On September 1, 1939, German forces invaded Poland. France and Britain declared war on Germany two days later. World War II had begun.

Hitler's Nazi army marched across Europe, occupying Austria, Belgium, France, Czechoslovakia, Poland, Holland, and Greece. Reaching Soviet Russia, the Nazis met their match in the fiercely resistant Soviet Red Army. In 1941, the German Sixth Army was forced to surrender. It was surrounded by the Soviet army. Badly weakened, Hitler and his army were finally destroyed by the Allied forces of Britain, the Soviet Union, and the United States in 1945. Defeated, Hitler committed suicide.

CHAPTER FOUR

THE COMMUNIST DICTATORSHIPS

This photograph shows Joseph Stalin, Soviet premier and secretary of the Communist Party, seated at his desk in his office in Moscow, Russia, around 1950.

Beginning in 1689 with Peter the Great, monarchs ruled Russia. Russia developed a thriving cultural community and became a world power. Its political structure included a noble upper class and an underclass of serfs, who the nobles treated more like slaves than peasants. However, royal rule began to decline with the coming of the Industrial Revolution.

In 1861, Czar Alexander II abolished serfdom. This did not produce significant improvements for the underclass. As Russia's economy shifted from agriculture to industry, the peasants became more active in their quest for rights. The Russian royalty was not ready to deal with changing ideas and conditions.

Lenin and the Foundation of Communist Russia

Around the turn of the twentieth century, a group of reformers created the Russian Socialist Democratic Party and began to address the plight of the Russian underclass. Vladimir Ilyich Lenin, a Russian political thinker and revolutionary, was among its leaders. The reformers were inspired by the philosophy of Karl Marx and Friedrich Engels.

Marx and Engels had published a groundbreaking work called *The Communist Manifesto* in 1848. In it, they outlined the views and agenda of the new

Many posters such as this one, which boasts in its title "The Vast Majority of the People of the Earth Approves of Our Politics of Peace," were used to win support for Lenin and the Bolsheviks (later called the Communist Party).

Communist movement and proposed a Communist Revolution in which social classes and private property would be abolished. They envisioned that as the Industrial Revolution developed, workers throughout the world would rebel against factory owners, aristocracy, or the bourgeoisie. The workers would set up what Lenin later described as a "dictatorship of the proletariat," which would put all

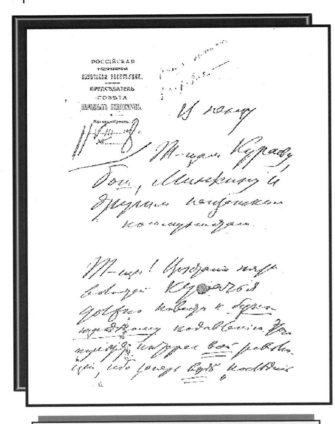

Russian leader Vladimir Lenin sent this letter, dated August 11, 1918, to Communists in Penza, Russia, ordering them to publicly hang 100 rich farmers—some of whom had rebelled against Communist policies—and to take away their grain to set an example that he would not tolerate opposition. (Refer to pages 55–56 for a transcription.)

property in collective ownership. The result would be a stateless, classless society. The dictatorship of the proletariat would exist only for the transition.

In 1903, the Socialist Democratic Party split into two rival factions: the Bolsheviks (Russian for "majority") and the Mensheviks (Russian for "minority"). Led by Lenin, the Bolsheviks were the more radical group, and they advocated an armed revolution against the czar.

The Russian Revolution of 1905 forced Czar Nicholas II into establishing a representative body, called a duma, with limited powers. Another revolution in February 1917, during World War I, caused the czar to give up his throne, yielding power to the duma. Dominated by Mensheviks, the duma appointed a provisional government. However, Lenin helped mastermind the October Revolution of 1917, overthrowing the provisional government. Lenin became the leader of Russia, and the Bolsheviks changed their name to the Communist Party.

The Communist Party declared the October Revolution as having created a dictatorship of the proletariat. Almost immediately, Lenin abolished private ownership of land and distributed confiscated land among the peasants. He also nationalized banks and established workers' control over factory production. Using the Cheka, a brutal police force, he began suppressing political opposition.

Lenin's coup led to the Russian civil war, which lasted until 1920. With the help of Leon Trotsky, Lenin emerged victorious. By 1922, Lenin had set up a one-party state. With himself as chief dictator, he turned the Communist Party into a dictatorship that controlled the hierarchy all the way down to the most local level.

The civil war had left the country in shambles. Lenin tried to revive the economy with his New Economic Policy (NEP) of 1921. It reintroduced aspects of capitalism into the Russian economy. In December 1922, he presided over the formation of the Union of Soviet Socialist Republics (USSR), which included Russia, Belarus, Ukraine, Armenia, Azerbaijan, and Georgia.

Meanwhile, a bitter rivalry arose between Trotsky and fellow Communist Joseph Stalin. Stalin had quickly risen in the ranks of the party and gained the powerful position of general secretary in 1922.

Lenin's health began to fail in 1922. During December and January 1923, he wrote a number of documents now known as his Last Testament. He noted, "Comrade Stalin, having become Secretary-General, has unlimited authority concentrated in his hands, and I am not sure whether he will always be capable of using that authority with sufficient caution." Lenin wanted Trotsky to be his successor. Lenin suffered a stroke in May and died on January 21, 1924.

Time magazine named Joseph Stalin Man of the Year for 1942, describing him as a hero. At the Battle of Stalingrad, a critical battle of World War II, Soviet forces defeated the Germans. The world did not yet know of Stalin's atrocities against his own people. Democracies did not yet view Communism as a dire threat. Here are some quotes from 1942 in which *Time* magazine defines the achievements of Stalin.

- "The year 1942 was a year of blood and strength. Only Joseph Stalin fully knew how close Russia stood to defeat in 1942, and only Joseph Stalin fully knew how he brought Russia through . . ."

- "He collectivized the farms and he built Russia into one of the four great industrial powers on earth. Stalin's methods were tough, but they paid off . . ."

- "What other war aims Stalin has are not officially known, but there are reports in high circles that he wants no new territories except at points needed to make Russia impregnable against invasion."

Stalin Takes Over

A few days after Lenin's death, Stalin made a speech filled with tributes. He emphasized Lenin's dedication to the dictatorship of the proletariat. "The dictatorship of the proletariat was established in our country on the basis of an alliance between the workers and peasants.

This is the first and fundamental basis of the Republic of Soviets." Nevertheless, he soon moved to consolidate power over the country into his own hands.

Stalin was quiet and orderly. Unlike Lenin, many of his Communist comrades did not see him as a serious threat. But as general secretary, he oversaw the organization of the entire party. He slowly filled positions of power with people loyal to him.

Stalin created a troika, or triumvirate, with Lev Kamenev and Grigory Zinovyev to oppose Trotsky. He began to denounce and arrest enemies who he claimed were disloyal to the party. Soon, however, Stalin slowly started undermining Kamenev and Zinovyev even as they continued to fight Trotsky. At last, the two joined with Trotsky in 1926 to try to halt Stalin's success. It was too late. In 1927, Kamenev lost his post and both Zinovyev and Trotsky were expelled from the Communist Party. By 1929, Stalin was the undisputed dictator of the USSR.

Reforms and Atrocities

In 1928, Stalin began his Five Year Plan, a program of industrialization and collectivization of farms. He seized land from the kulaks, or prosperous peasants. His forces drove families from their homes, deporting or killing them. Many people died of starvation. Collectivization was not successful at first. Famine spread across the USSR, eventually killing more than 14 million people. It took until 1935 for Russia to produce enough to feed her own people.

Stalin imposed quotas in industry. Business or factory workers that failed to reach the target were severely punished, even executed.

This cartoon of Joseph Stalin depicts him contemplating a paper that reads, "List of Thirteen Enemies Destroyed." The cartoon, published in 1939 (after Stalin's succession and prior to Germany's invasion), suggests that Stalin is looking to eliminate Russia's stumbling blocks.

Industry expanded through Stalin's years, but often factory workers worried more about the quota than the quality of the product. Stalin enacted a number of Five Year Plans during his rule.

People suspected of opposing Stalin would be executed or sent to labor camps called gulags. His secret police force, the NKVD (People's Commisariat for Internal Affairs), kept the people in constant fear. During the "purges" of the 1930s, millions of people disappeared. Stalin held show trials during which his old adversaries were forced to admit to horrific crimes they had not committed. Kamenev and Zinovyev were both executed after show trials.

Stalin feared Germany's growing power, and in 1939, he agreed to a non-aggression treaty with Germany. Germany invaded the USSR anyway in 1941, and Stalin joined the Allied forces (Great Britain and the United States) of World War II. The alliance fell apart after the war ended in 1945. Many countries followed the USSR's lead and adopted Communist governments. Democratic countries began to distrust countries run by Communists.

This poster shows Franklin D. Roosevelt, Winston Churchill, and Joseph Stalin as the three leaders who defeated Adolf Hitler. Roosevelt had a strong relationship with Stalin and referred to him as Papa Joe. However, Churchill was reluctant to trust their ally.

In 1946, British prime minister Winston Churchill delivered his famous Iron Curtain speech: "Nobody knows what Soviet Russia and its Communist international organization intends to do in

This poster shows Russians marching while Churchill and Uncle Sam (bottom right) look nervously behind them. It reads, "For a Stable Peace! Against Those Who Would Ignite a New War." Many feared that tensions between the United States and the Soviet Union would bring about more devastation.

the immediate future . . . an iron curtain has descended across the Continent." This rift between Communist and democratic countries led to the Cold War, a prolonged nonviolent state of hostility between the Soviet Union and the United States that lasted into the 1990s.

Stalin's repression of the Soviet people tightened after the end of World War II. The country had been devastated, and the Soviet people endured hard times while rebuilding. The government denounced leading artists, writers, and scientists. Stalin insisted that people revere him. He rewrote history books to portray himself as a great leader. Stalin controlled the USSR until his death in 1953.

CHAPTER FIVE

FRANCO AND FASCISM IN SPAIN

Stalin and Hitler led the two opposing ideologies that spread during the early twentieth century. Stalin's Communism stood for the end of private property and social classes. Hitler's Nazism stood for absolute power and Aryan supremacy. Fascism opposed everything Communism stood for. It supported nationalism and a powerful central government that allowed no opposing views. These two ideas came into direct conflict during the Spanish civil war of 1936 through 1939. At the end, the Fascist-supported dictator Francisco Franco took control of Spain.

General Francisco Franco is shown in full military attire in this 1954 photograph. Like most dictators, Franco kept strict control over the military during his rule of Spain.

POR LA
ESPAÑA
UNA GRANDE Y LIBRE

This poster, "For Spain, Great and Free," depicts a soldier waving the Falange flag. Falange, a Fascist political party, was formed in 1933 by José Antonio Primo de Rivera. In 1937, the party joined the Carlist militia and renamed itself Falange Español.

Spain had existed as a weak republic during the five years before the war. The government could not heal the divisions within Spanish society. Politically, people were split between right-wing parties, including the Fascists and others, and the left-wing Popular Front. The Popular Front consisted of Communists, anarchists, and Socialists, among others. George Orwell, the British writer and activist, described the Popular Front in his book *Homage to Catalonia*: "The Popular Front is in [essence] an alliance of enemies, and it seems probable that it must always end by one partner swallowing the other."

The government lost the support of landowners and the powerful Catholic Church. The church ran schools, hospitals, and soup kitchens for the poor. But throughout the nineteenth century, it had helped discourage the lower and middle classes from rebelling against the rich ruling class.

Leon Trotsky wrote about the struggle in a 1931 document ironically titled "Ten Commandments of the Spanish Communist." It called for "confiscation of all properties of the monarchy and the church for the benefit of the people, above all, for the unemployed and the poor peasants and for improving the conditions of the soldiers; complete separation of church and state." The Republican Union Party (RUP) in Spain passed policies that reduced the influence of the church.

In February 1936, the Populist Party won control of the Republican government. Violence worsened on both sides. The Falange Español, the Spanish Fascist party, committed acts of terrorism. Right-wing supporters and army officers began plotting to overthrow the government.

International Support for the Republic

The rebels attempted a coup on July 17, 1936. A significant portion of the Spanish military joined in the strike. Most important was the African army based in Spanish Morocco across the Strait of Gibraltar. General Francisco Franco led the African army.

The attempt at a quick overthrow failed, and the fighting stretched into a three-year civil war. Initially, the Movimiento Nacional, or National Movement, had few political aims beyond ousting the Republicans. The leaders saw that they would need outside help to win the conflict, and they turned to the Fascists of Italy and Germany. The Falange Español, a minor political party, had played only a small role in the July coup. Franco became commander in chief of the Nationalists in October 1936.

The world turned its eyes toward Spain. Fascism had recently gained hold in Germany, and many democratic governments feared that it could spread in Spain and other countries. But the

French, British, and other European governments chose a policy of nonintervention in the war. They worried that if their forces fought in Spain, the conflict would spread to include Germany. After World War I, they wanted to avoid war at any cost. Only Stalin actively helped the Republicans of Spain.

Private citizens, however, answered the Spanish Republicans' cry for help. Tens of thousands of volunteers from dozens of countries sneaked into Spain to fight. Many joined the International Brigades, organized by the Communist International organization. "I had come to Spain with some notion of writing newspaper articles, but I had joined the militia almost immediately, because at that time and in that atmosphere it seemed the only conceivable thing to do," wrote George Orwell. Some volunteers were veterans of World War I, but others came with no military experience. Americans formed the Abraham Lincoln Brigade. Internationally, intellectuals supported the Republicans and their fight against Fascism.

The Horrors of the Spanish Civil War

Many of the people fighting for the Republicans wanted above all else to oppose Fascism. Others hoped to bring about a Communist revolution. The Republican forces were disorganized and lacked a strong military strategy.

General Franco saw the war as a crusade to reinstate old Spanish traditions and values. He linked his fight strongly with the Catholic Church. The Nationalist supporters were put under strict military control, regardless of their various political loyalties.

Both sides committed atrocities that horrified the world. Prisoners were executed with no trial. Franco's Nationalists seized records of the Popular Front and political organizations, and made up "black lists" of enemies. Similarly, some parties fighting for the Republicans showed no mercy to anyone belonging to right-wing or church organizations. The Republican government could not rein in extremist militias and revolutionaries. In August 1936, the Nationalists rounded up and massacred 3,000 to 4,000 "enemies." In November, 2,000 political prisoners were shot and buried in mass graves in Republican-held territory. Republican fighters killed priests, burned churches, and destroyed sacred objects.

In April 1937, German planes, at Franco's request, bombed the small town of Guernica on market day. They turned the town into rubble and killed 1,500 people. On the day he heard of the bombing, Spanish-born artist Pablo Picasso began painting his famous *Guernica*. The stark painting, one of Picasso's most famous pieces, shows distorted figures twisted in anguish.

Spain Under Franco

The Nationalists won the war in 1939. Francisco Franco became dictator of Spain. He immediately acted to punish his opponents by passing the brutal Political Responsibilities Act. This policy allowed him to punish people for any anti-Nationalist actions during the war, even if they had been legal at the time. This included anyone who had "held directorial responsibility in one of the parties, groups, or associations belonging to the so-called Popular Front, or in parties or groups allied or associated with it, or in separatist organizations,

The Basque holy city of Guernica was devastated by war in 1937. The Basques, who live in four provinces of northern Spain and have no original relation to the Spanish, have managed to preserve their culture throughout hundreds of years.

or any organization opposing the victory of the National Movement." At least 28,000 people were executed. Some estimates claim that up to 150,000 people may have been killed. Hundreds of thousands more went into exile or were imprisoned.

With his background as a professional soldier, Franco viewed governance along military lines. He ruled Spain as the caudillo, or military leader. Spain was under martial law in the first nine years of his rule, during which he tried to erase virtually all traces of the parliamentary democracy that had existed before the civil war. In addition to being general of the Spanish military, Franco was also chief of state and head of government. Accordingly, he was the law. He ruled by decree and used the army to maintain order. He frequently declared state of emergencies during which he suspended what little civil liberties he allowed. Franco outlawed all political bodies except for the National Movement and limited suffrage, or the right to vote. Throughout much of his rule, he outlawed strikes and labor unions, and called in his military to suppress organized labor activities.

Francisco Franco meets with Italy's Benito Mussolini on March 4, 1944. Despite their friendship, Franco kept Spain neutral during World War II. He maintained this friendship even after the Italian dictator was toppled from power in 1943.

Franco ruled until his death in 1975. He cannily played factions of his party against each other so that they would not join against him. He gave the Catholic Church a prominent role in guiding the country.

Despite Franco's link to Hitler and Fascism, Spain remained a non-combatant during World War II. Spain joined the United Nations in 1955. Beginning in the 1960s, Franco relaxed labor laws, ended censorship, and allowed some other progressive measures. After his death, Spain made a smooth transition to democracy.

CHAPTER SIX

THREE DICTATORS OF THE AMERICAS

In the mid-twentieth century, political and economic turmoil in several countries in the Americas gave rise to a number of dictators in the region. Among the most notable of these are Cuba's Fidel Castro, Haiti's François "Papa Doc" Duvalier, and Chile's Augusto Pinochet.

Fidel Castro

In 1959, Cuban revolutionaries overturned the corrupt government of Fulgencio Batista. Fidel Castro emerged to become prime minister of Cuba. Distrusting the United States, Castro seized U.S.-owned property during his first year in power. The United States

Haitian president François Duvalier is shown in battle dress in his office on July 29, 1958, after his army put down a rebel attack. Duvalier took an active part in the military operation.

This poster, "Long Live Cuba, Territory Free from America," shows Cuban leader Fidel Castro triumphantly holding up a gun. Relations between the United States and Cuba disintegrated during the Cold War when Cuba became a threat to the United States. On the right is an aerial view of the Mariel naval port showing evidence of Soviet missiles being loaded. The Mariel naval port was the first site in Cuba to receive shipments of nuclear warheads from the USSR. The Soviet Union was the biggest contributor to the Cuban arsenal.

established an embargo, blocking trade with Cuba. Castro allied himself with the USSR. In 1961, he canceled elections, suspended the constitution, and proclaimed Cuba a Socialist nation.

Amid growing tension, American president John F. Kennedy attempted to invade Cuba in 1961. Now known as the Bay of Pigs invasion, this effort failed miserably. Cubans condemned the United States and rallied behind Castro.

In this letter, dated October 24, 1962, Soviet president Nikita Khrushchev warns President Kennedy not to set up a blockade of Cuba or to interfere with Soviet ships headed there. Khrushchev declares that such actions by the United States could lead to nuclear war. Kennedy blockaded the island anyway, and Khrushchev removed the Soviet missiles from Cuba. (Refer to pages 56–57 for a partial transcription.)

Castro allowed Soviet premier Nikita Khrushchev to place long-range nuclear missiles on Cuba. CIA surveillance planes discovered them on October 14, 1962, sparking the Cuban Missile Crisis.

Kennedy told the public about the missiles in a television address on October 22. He announced that the United States would prevent any ship carrying weapons to reach Cuba. Unwilling to spark a possible nuclear war, Khrushchev agreed on October 28 to withdraw the missiles.

Throughout the Cold War, Castro supported revolutionary movements elsewhere. When Communism fell in countries throughout the world in 1989, many Cubans tried to revolt. Cuba's economy faced a crisis, but Castro held on to power.

In 2002, Jimmy Carter visited Cuba. It was the first visit by a former or sitting president since Castro took office. Despite his visit, Cuba has not made any steps toward democracy, and the United States has not lifted the trade embargo.

François Duvalier

The people of Haiti elected Dr. François Duvalier president in September 1957. Haitians, living in one of the world's poorest countries, hoped that Duvalier would bring stability and prosperity to Haiti. He had overcome formidable obstacles in becoming a doctor and had worked in the countryside with poor Haitians. People considered him a humanitarian.

But Papa Doc, as he called himself, became a brutal dictator, ruling Haiti with an iron fist. He repressed all political opposition soon after taking office and had himself named president for life in 1964. He organized a personal secret police force called the Tontons

Pictured above are remnants of the victims of the Tontons Macoutes, also referred to as the death squad. Since there were so many fatalities under Duvalier, mass graves were used to dispose of the bodies.

Macoutes, named for a mythical Haitian boogeyman who grabs people and makes them vanish. They tortured and killed anyone thought to be Duvalier's enemy. Up to 40,000 Haitians were killed by the Tontons Macoutes. Others fled the country in droves.

MODERN DICTATORS

During the second half of the twentieth century, repressive dictatorships arose in a number of countries. Most occurred in poor nations or at a time of governmental and economic crisis. Here is a list of some of the most notorious dictators.

Saddam Hussein

Argentina Juan Perón, 1946–1955
The "Generals," 1976–1983

Cambodia Pol Pot, 1975–1979

China Mao Tse-tung, 1949–1976

Indonesia Suharto, 1976–1998

Iran Ayatollah Ruholla Khomeini, 1979–1988

Iraq Saddam Hussein, 1979–2003

Libya Muammar Qaddafi, 1969–

North Korea Kim Il Sung, 1948–1994
Kim Jong Il, 1994–

Philippines Ferdinand Marcos, 1972–1986

Romania Nicolae Ceausescu, 1965–1989

Uganda Idi Amin, 1971–1979

Ayatollah Khomeini

Idi Amin

In 1963, a Haitian electrical worker described Haitians' desperate life under Duvalier. "Duvalier has performed an economic miracle. He has taught us to live without money, to eat without food . . . to live without life."

The United States took no action to depose Duvalier. The American government, concerned at the time with the suppression of Communism, ignored Haiti's horrific dictator. Castro's Communist regime worried American leaders more than Duvalier's bloody rule. Duvalier's dictatorship prevented Communism from gaining a hold in the country.

After Duvalier's death in 1971, Jean-Claude "Baby Doc" Duvalier took control of the country, following in his father's repressive footsteps. The Duvalier regime lasted until Jean-Claude went into exile in 1986.

Augusto Pinochet

In 1970, Salvador Allende became the first democratically elected Socialist president in Latin America. Opposed by two other candidates, he received about 37 percent of the Chilean vote. Allende tried to transform Chile into a Socialist nation. He nationalized banks and many private industries, and instituted a land reform program.

Other branches of the government, the military, and the wealthy landowners of Chile resisted his measures. The United States, opposed to any Socialist regime, also helped block Allende's policies. Chile's economy crashed. Chileans faced food shortages and high prices, the result of inflation. Striking workers held violent demonstrations.

On September 11, 1973, the military led a revolt and stormed the Moneda, Chile's presidential palace. Salvador Allende made a last radio broadcast as planes bombed the palace. Allende was found shot after the coup, and his death was declared a suicide.

General Augusto Pinochet installed himself as dictator. He immediately suspended the constitution and arrested thousands of his political opponents. Many Chileans were tortured or killed, while others simply "disappeared." Pinochet reversed Allende's economic measures with mixed results. He banned political parties and imposed strict censorship.

Miguel Littín, one of Chile's foremost filmmakers, fled the country after Pinochet's coup. In 1985, he defied the ban on returning. Disguised as an Uruguayan businessman, he made a film about Pinochet's Chile. The Nobel Prize–winning author Gabriel García Márquez described the adventure in *Clandestine in Chile*, telling the story from Littín's point of view. Littín had not seen his homeland for fifteen years. Márquez writes:

> As we approached the center of the city, I stopped admiring the material splendor with which the dictatorship sought to cover the blood of tens of thousands killed or disappeared, and ten times that number driven into exile, and instead concentrated on the people in view. They were walking unusually fast, perhaps because curfew was so close.

In 1988, Chileans voted not to extend Pinochet's term beyond 1990. Free elections in 1989 began a fairly smooth transition back to democracy.

Dictatorships in the World

Napoléon rose to power after the French Revolution because he appeared to be a champion of equality and peace. Hitler appealed to the downtrodden Germans' sense of nationalism. Stalin's totalitarianism gave workers hope for the future of their society. But along the way, they and other dictators turned to intimidation and violence to suppress and control those they dominated. While dictators such as Caesar and Napoléon have left legacies of achievement, they and other dictators assembled vast armies to crush the lives of millions.

To rule absolutely, a dictator shuts down the former government. He curtails the rights of those he rules, forcing them into submission through propaganda, abuse, and brutality. Dictators take what they want, leaving those they control to suffer dislocation, poverty, pain, and often death. When dictators are finally removed, they leave behind a country or empire in ruins.

TIMELINE

46 BC	Julius Caesar becomes dictator of Rome.
44 BC	A group of Roman senators assassinates Caesar.
1793–1794	Maximilien Robespierre controls France during the Reign of Terror.
1804	Napoléon Bonaparte is crowned emperor of France.
1928	Joseph Stalin begins his first Five Year Plan in the USSR.
1933	Adolf Hitler becomes chancellor of Germany.
1939	Francisco Franco takes control of Spain after Nationalists win the Spanish civil war.
	World War II begins.
1945	World War II ends with Germany's defeat.
1961	Fidel Castro suspends elections and proclaims Cuba a Socialist nation.
1962	Cuban Missile Crisis.
1964	François "Papa Doc" Duvalier becomes president for life of Haiti.
1971	Papa Doc Duvalier dies in office; his son Jean-Claude "Baby Doc" Duvalier assumes the presidency.
1973	Augusto Pinochet deposes Chilean president Salvador Allende in a military coup.
1988	Chileans vote not to extend Pinochet's term in office beyond 1990.
2003	Saddam Hussein's regime toppled by U.S. invasion of Iraq.

Page 28: Excerpt from Reinhard Heydrich's November 10, 1938, letter to German police departments regarding anti-Jewish demonstrations

SECRET!

To all

Headquarters and Stations of the State (Political) Police

Urgent! For immediate attention of Chief and his deputy!

Re: Measures Against the Jews Tonight.

Because of the assassination of Legation Secretary vom Rath in Paris, demonstrations throughout the Reich are to be expected tonight—November 9 to 10, 1938. The following orders are issued for dealing with these occurances . . .

b) Stores and residences of Jews may only be destroyed but not looted. The police are instructed to supervise compliance with this order and to arrest looters.

c) Special care is to be taken on commercial streets that non-Jewish businesses are completely secured against damage.

Page 32: Letter from Lenin to his associates in 1918

11-8-18

Send to Penza

To Comrades Kuraev,
Bosh, Minkin and
other Penza
communists

Comrades! The revolt by the five kulak volosts must be suppressed without mercy. The interest of the entire revolution demands this, because we have now before us our final decisive battle "with the kulaks." We need to set an example.

1) You need to hang (hang without fail, so that the public sees) at least 100 notorious kulaks, the rich, and the bloodsuckers.
2) Publish their names.
3) Take away all of their grain.
4) Execute the hostages—in accordance with yesterday's telegram.

This needs to be accomplished in such a way, that people for hundreds of miles around will see, tremble, know and scream out: let's choke and strangle those blood-sucking kulaks.

Telegraph us acknowledging receipt and execution of this.

Yours, Lenin

P.S. Use your toughest people for this.

TRANSLATOR'S COMMENTS: Lenin uses the derogative term kulak in reference to the class of prosperous peasants. A volost was a territorial/administrative unit consisting of a few villages and surrounding land.

Page 48: Excerpt from Nikita Khrushchev's October 24, 1962, letter to President John F. Kennedy
Excellency
Mr. John F. Kennedy
President of the United States of America
Washington

Dear Mr. President,

Imagine, Mr. President, what if we were to present to you such an ultimatum as you have presented to us by your actions. How would you react to it? I think you would be outraged at such a move on our part. And this we would understand . . .

You, Mr. President, are not declaring a quarantine, but rather issuing an ultimatum, and you are threatening that if we do not obey your orders, you will then use force. Think about what you are saying! And you want to persuade me to agree to this! What does it mean to agree to these demands? It would mean for us to conduct our relations with other countries not by reason, but by yielding to tyranny. You are not appealing to reason; you want to intimidate us.

No, Mr. President, I cannot agree to this, and I think that deep inside, you will admit that I am right. I am convinced that if you were in my place you would do the same. . .

Therefore, Mr. President, if you weigh the present situation with a cool head without giving way to passion, you will understand that the Soviet Union cannot afford not to decline the despotic demands of the USA. When you lay conditions such as these before us, try to put yourself in our situation and consider how the USA would react to such conditions. I have no doubt that if anyone attempted to dictate similar conditions to you—the United States—you would reject such an attempt. And we likewise say no.

The Soviet government considers the violation of the freedom of navigation in international waters and air space to constitute an act of aggression propelling humankind into the abyss of a world nuclear-missile war. Therefore, the Soviet government cannot instruct captains of Soviet ships bound for Cuba to observe orders of American naval forces blockading this island. Our instructions to Soviet sailors are to observe strictly the generally accepted standards of navigation in international waters and not retreat one step from them. And, if the American side violates these rights, it must be aware of the responsibility it will bear for this act. To be sure, we will not remain mere observers of pirate actions by American ships in the open sea. We will then be forced on our part to take those measures we deem necessary and sufficient to defend our rights. To this end we have all that is necessary.

Respectfully,
/s/ N. Khrushchev
N. KHRUSHCHEV
Moscow
24 October 1962

GLOSSARY

abdicate To formally give up something, particularly a high office.

anarchist A person who believes that all governments and laws are unnatural.

artillery Large guns manned by crews.

censorship The examination and suppression of information considered dangerous or objectionable.

collectivization The idea of placing land and the means of production under group control.

Communism A form of government whose ideology is based on a classless society in which all private property, land, and factories are owned by all of a nation's people.

coup A sudden takeover of leadership or power.

empire A state and its territory, or a number of states, controlled by a single ruler.

faction A group forming a minority within a larger group and working toward a common cause.

Fascism A form of government in which a person or group rules through strict control.

führer A German word for "leader" that has commonly come to mean "tyrant."

guillotine A device used for beheading people by dropping a heavy blade onto their necks.

ideology A set of beliefs that reflects the needs and desires of a group or nation.

magistrate In the Roman Empire, officials who administered justice in Rome's colonies.

orator A public speaker.

propaganda Information distributed by the advocates or opponents of a cause and designed to persuade the public to accept their beliefs.

revolutionary One who seeks to bring about major changes in society or government.

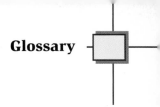

Socialism A form of government in which the people share many things, but private property still exists.

sovereign A supreme authority.

Third Reich Hitler's name for Germany during his rule. He considered the Holy Roman Empire the First Reich and the German Empire lasting from 1871 to 1918 to be the Second Reich. He used the phrase to link his reign historically to the times when Germany had been a great power.

triumvirate Government by three high-ranking officials.

FOR MORE INFORMATION

Web Sites
Due to the changing nature of Internet links, the Rosen Publishing Group, Inc., has developed an online list of Web sites related to the subject of this book. This site is updated regularly. Please use this link to access the list:

http://www.rosenlinks.com/psps/dict

FOR FURTHER READING

Giblin, James Cross. *The Life and Death of Adolf Hitler*. New York: Clarion Books, 2002.

Green, Robert. *Julius Caesar.* New York: Franklin Watts, Inc., 1996.

Henderson, Harry, ed. *The Age of Napoleon.* San Diego: Lucent Books, 1999.

Ingram, Scott. *Joseph Stalin*. Woodbridge, CT: Blackbirch Marketing, 2002.

Katz, William Loren, and Marc Crawford. *The Lincoln Brigade: A Picture History*. New York: Atheneum, 1989.

Press, Petra. *Fidel Castro: An Unauthorized Biography*. Chicago: Heinemann Library, 2000.

BIBLIOGRAPHY

Abel, Theodore. *Why Hitler Came Into Power*. Cambridge, MA: Harvard University Press, 1986.

Arthur, Charles. *Haiti: A Guide to the People, Politics and Culture*. New York: Interlink Books, 2002.

De Jonge, Alex. *Stalin, and the Shaping of the Soviet Union*. New York: Quill, 1986.

García Márquez, Gabriel. *Clandestine in Chile: The Adventures of Miguel Littín*. New York: Henry Holt and Company, 1986.

Herold, Christopher. *The Age of Napoleon*. New York: American Heritage Publishing Co., Inc., 1963.

Lovell, Sarah, ed. *Leon Trotsky Speaks*. New York: Pathfinder Press, 1972.

Neumann, Franz. *Notes on the Theory of Dictatorship. The Democratic and Authoritarian State; Essays in Political and Legal Theory*. Herbert Marcuse, ed. Glencoe, IL: Free Press, 1957.

Orwell, George. *Homage to Catalonia*. New York: Harcourt Brace and Company, 1952.

Ranzato, Gabriele. *The Spanish Civil War*. New York: Interlink Books, 1999.

Roberts, Timothy R. *Ancient Rome*. New York: MetroBooks, 2000.

Rudé, George, ed. *Robespierre*. Englewood Cliffs, NJ: Prentice-Hall, Inc., 1967.

Shirer, William L. *The Rise and Fall of the Third Reich*. New York: Crest Books, 1962.

Trotsky, Leon. *The Spanish Revolution (1931–39)*. New York: Pathfinder Press, 1973.

PRIMARY SOURCE IMAGE LIST

Pages 4–5: Undated photograph of Augusto Pinochet reviewing troops. Taken by Martin Thomas.

Page 14: *Napoléon on Horseback at the St. Bernard Pass*, painting by Jacques-Louis David, 1801.

Page 17: Print depicting the interrogation of Robespierre, circa 1900. Housed at the Library of Congress Prints and Photographs Division in Washington, D.C.

Page 19: Painting of Napoléon, created between 1905 and 1915. Housed at the Library of Congress Prints and Photographs Division in Washington, D.C.

Page 22: Photograph of Adolf Hitler, 1934.

Page 25: Nazi propaganda poster urging Germans to support German products. Created by Günther W. Nagel between 1932 and 1945. Housed at the Library of Congress Prints and Photographs Division in Washington, D.C.

Page 26: Photograph of Adolf Hitler addressing a rally in Dortmund, Germany, in 1933.

Page 28: November 10, 1938, letter from Reinhard Heydrich, Nazi chief of the security police, to police departments. Housed at the United States Holocaust Memorial Museum in Washington, D.C.

Page 29: October 9, 1934, photograph of Benito Mussolini.

Page 30: Photograph of Joseph Stalin, circa 1950.

Page 31: "The Vast Majority of the People of the Earth Approves of Our Politics of Peace." Undated Communist poster bearing the image of Vladimir Lenin. Housed at the Library of Congress Prints and Photographs Division in Washington, D.C.

Page 32: August 11, 1918, letter from Vladimir Lenin to Communists in Penza, Russia, ordering the public hanging of 100 rich farmers. Housed at the Library of Congress in Washington, D.C.

Page 36: "Unlucky Number." Satirical drawing by Lute Pease, created between 1933 and 1939. Housed at the Library of Congress Prints and Photographs Division in Washington, D.C.

Page 37: "For Equal Rights to All Nations. The Three Men Who Saved the World." Poster, circa 1945. Housed at the Library of Congress Prints and Photographs Division in Washington, D.C.

Page 38: "For a Stable Peace! Against Those Who Would Ignite a New War." Communist propaganda poster, 1949. Housed at the Library of Congress Prints and Photographs Division in Washington, D.C.

Page 39: Photograph of Francisco Franco, 1954.

Page 40: "For Spain, Great and Free." Falange propaganda poster, 1936. Housed at the Library of Congress Prints and Photographs Division in Washington, D.C.

Page 44: May 8, 1837, photograph of Spanish city of Guernica after it was bombed by German aircraft.

Page 45: Photograph of Francisco Franco and Benito Mussolini, taken on March 4, 1944.

Page 46: Photograph of François Duvalier, taken in Port-au-Prince, Haiti, on July 29, 1958.

Page 47 (left): "Long Live Cuba, Territory Free from America." Cuban poster, 1968. Housed at the Library of Congress Prints and Photographs Division in Washington, D.C.

Page 47 (right): Photograph showing aerial view of Mariel naval port in Cuba during the Cuban Missile Crisis, 1962. Housed at the Library of Congress in Washington, D.C.

Page 48: October 24, 1962, letter from Nikita Khrushchev to John F. Kennedy. Housed at the Library of Congress in Washington, D.C.

Page 49: January 1986 photograph of human skulls at a mass gravesite near Port-au-Prince, Haiti. Taken by Bill Gentile.

Page 50 (top): Photograph of Saddam Hussein, 1981.

Page 50 (middle): Photograph of Ayatollah Khomeini, February 1979.

Page 50 (bottom): Photograph of General Idi Amin, circa 1972.

INDEX

ABOUT THE AUTHOR
Rose McCarthy is a freelance writer who lives in Chicago, Illinois.

Designer: Nelson Sá; **Editor:** Wayne Anderson;
Photo Researcher: Hillary Arnold